S.P.I.R.E.®

Specialized Program Individualizing Reading Excellence

3rd Edition

Workbook

Level 6

Sheila Clark-Edmands

EDUCATORS PUBLISHING SERVICE

Cambridge and Toronto

Editorial Project Manager: Tracey Newman
Senior Editor: Laura A. Woollett
Assistant Editor: Rachel L. Smith

© 2012 by Educators Publishing Service. All rights reserved. No part of this book may be reproduced or utilized in any form or by any electronic or mechanical means, including photocopying, without permission in writing from the publisher.

Printed in Benton Harbor, MI, in June 2016
ISBN 978-0-8388-5721-2

5 6 7 8 9 PPG 20 19 18 17 16

| asleep | aboard | afraid |
| alike | about | aloud |

Write a word from above on the line.

____

____

____

____

Fill in each blank with a word from above.

1. The conductor yelled, "All _______________."

2. The twins looked exactly _______________.

3. The small child fell _______________ in his mom's arms.

4. Mom read the book _______________.

Put together:

a + sleep _______________   a + like _______________

a + board _______________   a + loud _______________

| opera | banana | camera | parka | orca | gorilla |
| extra | awhile | away | polka | umbrella | panda |

Write a word from above on the line.

__________________________   __________________________

__________________________   __________________________

Fill in each blank with a word from the box.

1. We went to the _________________ to hear the singer.

2. Alan packed a _________________ for his trip to Alaska.

3. A _________________ bear has big black and white markings.

4. I let the balloon go, and it sailed _________________.

5. Would you like this _________________ ticket to the baseball game?

6. Can you stay _________________ and have dinner?

S.P.I.R.E.® Level 6 © SSI • Do Not Copy

Put together:

fix + able ___________________

re + charge + able ___________________

man + age + able ___________________

ad + just + able ___________________

en + force + able ___________________

com + fort + able ___________________

hug + ga + ble ___________________

move + able ___________________

Fill in each blank with a word from above.

1. The cute little child was ___________________.
2. The battery was ___________________.
3. The old, broken van was not ___________________.
4. The rule did not work because it was not ___________________.
5. My old sneakers are so ___________________ that I wear them every day.
6. Training our dog made her ___________________. Now she comes when we call.
7. The desk chair is ___________________.
8. The airplane model had six ___________________ parts.

S.P.I.R.E.® Level 6 © SSI • Do Not Copy

Box the prefix *a-*, ending *a-*, or suffix *-able.* Then say the word and read its meaning.

abound	to be in great numbers
ajar	a little bit open
abide	to put up with; tolerate
enforceable	able to be enforced or carried out
opera	a play that is sung

Choose a word from the box to replace the underlined word(s) in each sentence.

1. ___________________ That law is simply not <u>able to be carried out</u>.
2. ___________________ Who left the door <u>open</u>?
3. ___________________ Chen cannot <u>tolerate</u> this frigid weather.
4. ___________________ We saw a(n) <u>play</u> called The Magic Flute.
5. ___________________ Acorns <u>appear in great numbers</u> in the fall.

Complete each sentence with a word from the box.

1. Tamara has season tickets to the ___________________.
2. Cam did not shut the car door. He left it ___________________.
3. A good rule must be ___________________.
4. Ms. Jones will not ___________________ any bullies in the classroom.
5. Wildflowers will ___________________ in the field this spring.

S.P.I.R.E.® Level 6 © SSI • Do Not Copy

What Is Groundhog Day?

1. A "custom" is a common practice. Discuss the custom of celebrating Groundhog Day.

    ____

    ____

    ____

    ____

2. What are your thoughts on whether or not the groundhog can predict the weather?

    ____

    ____

    ____

    ____

3. List at least two other animals that hibernate in winter.

    ____

    ____

4. Write a letter to the Chamber of Commerce in Punxsutawney, Pennsylvania, and ask them to send you some information on Groundhog Day.

S.P.I.R.E.® Level 6 © SSI • Do Not Copy

Box the prefix *a-,* ending *-a,* or suffix *-able.* Then say the word and read its meaning.

amuse	to entertain in a playful way
loveable	easy to love
chargeable	able to be charged or powered
among	with or near; surrounded by
orca	a killer whale

Choose a word from the box to replace the underlined word(s) in each sentence.

1. _________________ Dad only uses batteries that are <u>able to be charged</u>.

2. _________________ Did you know that the <u>killer whale</u> is very peaceful?

3. _________________ We can count on Tam to <u>make us laugh</u>.

4. _________________ Pablo was <u>surrounded by</u> his best friends.

5. _________________ Jane has the most <u>easy-to-love</u> puppy.

Complete each sentence with a word from the box.

1. When the power goes out, it is helpful to have a _________________ flashlight.

2. That joke did not _________________ me.

3. I am lucky to have such a _________________ family.

4. Amar watched the kitten sleep _________________ his littermates.

5. The great _________________ leaped from the water.

S.P.I.R.E.® Level 6 © SSI • Do Not Copy

How Punxsutawney Phil
Came to Be

1. Is this story real or not real? How do you know?

____

____

____

2. What was Greg's problem?

____

____

3. How did the other groundhogs feel about him? Why?

____

____

4. How did Greg solve his problem?

____

____

5. Write about your favorite part of the story.

____

____

____

____

____

S.P.I.R.E.® Level 6 © SSI • Do Not Copy

Box the prefix *a-*, ending *-a*, or suffix *-able.* Then say the word and read its meaning.

<table>
<tr><td>huggable</td><td>pleasant to hug</td></tr>
<tr><td>amuck</td><td>in a jumbled or wild manner</td></tr>
<tr><td>await</td><td>to wait for</td></tr>
<tr><td>changeable</td><td>able to change</td></tr>
<tr><td>agenda</td><td>a list of things to be done; a plan</td></tr>
</table>

Choose a word from the box to replace the underlined word(s) in each sentence.

1. The big stuffed bear was soft and ___________________.
2. What is the ________________ for this meeting?
3. I ________________ your message.
4. The bookshelf is ________________. You can move the shelves.
5. The energetic puppies ran ________________ in the dog park.

Add *-able* to make new words. Cross out the final *e* or double the final consonant, if necessary.

1. The broken van is fix________.
2. Someone who agrees with you is agree________.
3. If the story seems real, it is believe________.
4. A small puppy is love________.
5. If you can depend on a person, they are depend________.

S.P.I.R.E.® Level 6 © SSI • Do Not Copy

The Shark

1. List three ways a shark differs from a fish.

   ____

   ____

   ____

2. Why is the shark called the "perfect hunter"?

   ____

   ____

   ____

3. Label the shark by using the words in the box.

jaws	dorsal fin	gills	lateral line

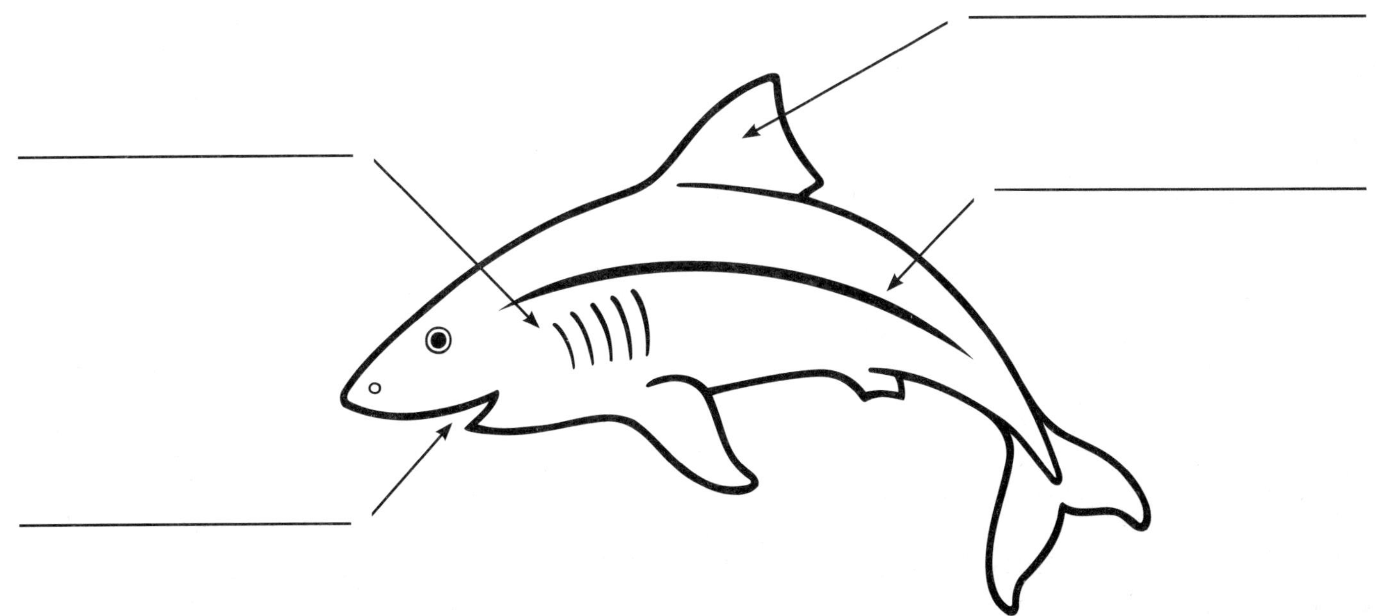

S.P.I.R.E.® Level 6 © SSI • Do Not Copy

Box the prefix *a-*, ending *-a*, or suffix *-able*. Then say the word and read its meaning.

parka	a type of jacket
dependable	trustworthy
panda	a type of bear
abandon	to leave or forsake
manageable	easy to manage

Choose a word from the box to replace the underlined word(s) in the sentence.

1. _________________ Zip up your <u>jacket</u>.
2. _________________ The <u>large bear</u> eats bamboo leaves.
3. _________________ When it's hot, my hair is not <u>easy to control</u>.
4. _________________ He will <u>leave behind</u> this project to start another.
5. _________________ Lilly is a <u>trustworthy</u> pal.

Complete each sentence with a word from the box.

1. Mike never forgets things; he is very _________________.
2. If you can manage something, it is _________________.
3. A _________________ is a large bear.
4. Jerry would never _________________ his new kitten.
5. Dara's _________________ kept her warm and dry.

S.P.I.R.E.® Level 6 © SSI • Do Not Copy

Kinds of Sharks

basking sharks	nurse sharks
whale sharks	megamouth sharks
lantern sharks	angel sharks
hammerhead sharks	

Match the name with the shark.

______________________ 1. These deep-sea sharks glow in the dark. They can also flash their lights to attract things to eat.

______________________ 2. These tricky sharks hide under the sand on the sea floor. They have wide fins that look like wings.

______________________ 3. These are the largest of all sharks and can grow to 50–60 feet. They are peaceful and slow.

______________________ 4. These sharks are odd-looking. Their heads are shaped like the end of a hammer.

______________________ 5. Not many of these sharks have been seen. Their smiles are three feet long.

Draw a picture of one kind of shark.

S.P.I.R.E.® Level 6 © SSI • Do Not Copy

 Circle ten things that describe what you know about sharks.

have small pores in head to find electric current of fish

several rows of teeth

cannot smell

have swim bladder filled with air

keen sense of smell

one row of teeth

most loved sea animal

skin is soft

has a lateral line to pick up sound and movement

called the perfect hunter

come in one size

must keep swimming

do not have bones

covered with small, sharp, tooth-like scales

see best in dim light

make good pets

likes bright lights

S.P.I.R.E.® Level 6 © SSI • Do Not Copy

dolphin	graph	telephone	sphere	gopher
microphone	photograph	pamphlets	cell phone	trophy

Write the word on the line.

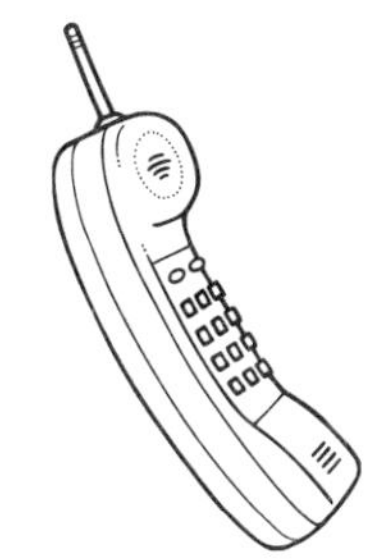

____

____

____

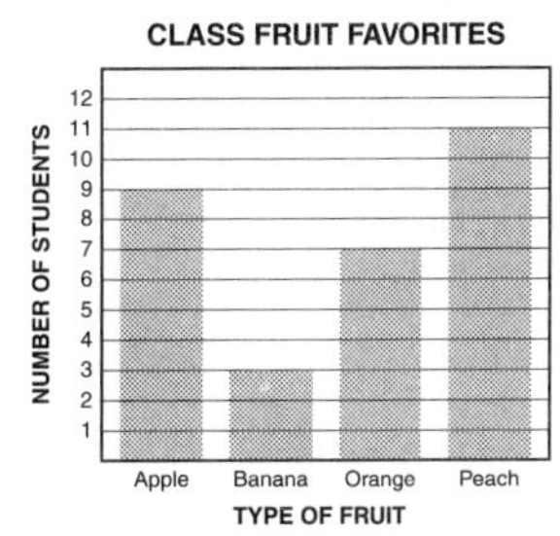

____

____

____

Fill in each blank with a word from the box.

1. Sing into the ______________________.

2. A ______________________ is round on all sides like a ball.

3. We handed out ______________________ advertising the school play.

S.P.I.R.E.® Level 6 © SSI • Do Not Copy

Write each word in the correct box.

Phyllis   dolphin   cell phone   Ralph

telegraph   pamphlet   Phil   telephone

elephant   alphabet   sphere   gopher

trophy   Phillip   microphone

<table>
<tr><td>

Animals

____

____

____

</td><td>

Ways to Communicate

____

____

____

____

____

____

</td></tr>
<tr><td>

Names

____

____

____

____

</td><td>

</td></tr>
</table>

S.P.I.R.E.® Level 6 © SSI • Do Not Copy

The Phantom of Room Twelve

1. How could the children tell which plants belonged to them?

   ____

   ____

2. How did the children use what they learned in math to find out about the plants?

   ____

   ____

3. What was the problem, and who first discovered it?

   ____

   ____

4. What happened after the problem was discovered?

   ____

   ____

5. How was the problem solved?

   ____

   ____

6. What did the children learn about getting along?

   ____

   ____

S.P.I.R.E.® Level 6 © SSI • Do Not Copy

Sometimes authors use certain words to help you see in your mind what you are reading. The literal meanings of these descriptions do not always make sense. Read each description below and circle the correct meaning.

1. The class was so silent, you could <u>hear a pin drop</u>.
   a. The children made little ringing sounds, like a telephone.
   b. The children did not make any sound.
   c. The pin woke everyone up, like when a phone rings at night.

2. When the teacher asked who passed the note, it was hard not to tell her as she looked at us with <u>hawk eyes</u>.
   a. Her eyes were shaped like spheres.
   b. Her eyes were as big as an elephant's.
   c. She looked at us carefully as if she could read our minds.

3. The fog came in on <u>little cat feet</u>.
   a. The fog came in with a loud sound.
   b. The fog came in very quietly.
   c. The fog came in very fast.

4. The wind sounded like <u>thousands of howling wolves</u>.
   a. The wind was fierce and wild.
   b. The wind was gentle and warm.
   c. The wind swirled in the shape of a sphere.

5. I had to <u>twist my friend's arm</u> to get her to go with me.
   a. I hurt her arm.
   b. I had to drag her by the arm so she would go.
   c. I had to beg and beg her to go, and she finally did.

S.P.I.R.E.® Level 6 © SSI • Do Not Copy

Circle all the words with *ph* and write them on the lines below.

1. The singer held a microphone.
2. The gopher burrowed into the ground.
3. The child was printing the alphabet.
4. The man held a cell phone.
5. The telephone was ringing.
6. The child rode the elephant.
7. Phillip held a trophy.
8. Phyllis looked at the pamphlet.
9. The child watched the dolphin in the tank.
10. Phyllis held her trophy up so everyone could see it.
11. The class graphed the change in temperature during the year.
12. Phillip is a member of the track team.
13. A typhoon is a kind of storm that happens at sea.
14. Alana got a part-time job at the pharmacy.
15. Every one should complete a physical activity during the day.

________________________   ________________________

________________________   ________________________

________________________   ________________________

________________________   ________________________

________________________   ________________________

________________________   ________________________

________________________   ________________________

S. P.I.R.E.® Level 6 © SSI • Do Not Copy

The Inventor of the Telephone

1. How did Bell's family influence his interest in communicating?

   ____

   ____

   ____

2. Why do you think Bell did poorly in some subjects in school?

   ____

   ____

   ____

3. How did Bell's grandfather make him interested in improving himself?

   ____

   ____

   ____

4. Bell went to Boston, Massachusetts to teach at a school for the deaf. How did this turn out to be a good move?

   ____

   ____

   ____

S.P.I.R.E.® Level 6 © SSI • Do Not Copy

5. When Bell was working on transmitting sounds, what weakness
    did he have that made his work slow and difficult? How did he
    solve this problem?

    ____

    _______________________________   _________________________

    ____

    ____

6. Was Bell the only person at that time working on inventing the
    telephone? Explain.

    ____

    ____

    ____

    ____

7. How did Bell's life turn out? What kind of person would you say
    Bell was?

    ____

    ____

    ____

    ____

8. How was Bell honored when he passed away?

    ____

    ____

    ____

 A hobby is something you pursue during free time for enjoyment. Circle all the activities that could be a hobby. Cross out the activities that could not be a hobby.

photography

puzzles

homework

talking on the phone

learning the alphabet

teaching children the alphabet

singing into a microphone

writing

commuting

building your own telegraph

looking at elephants at the zoo

flying

winning trophies

chasing gophers

surfing

writing pamphlets

cleaning

calculating the area of a sphere

S.P.I.R.E.® Level 6 © SSI • Do Not Copy

Pheasants

1. What is the most photographed bird? Hint: it is a relation of the pheasant.

   ____

   ____

2. Describe the pheasant's habitat.

   ____

   ____

3. How are pheasants unlike most other birds?

   ____

   ____

4. How does the male pheasant act to attract a mate?

   ____

   ____

5. What does the saying "proud as a peacock" mean?

   ____

   ____

   ____

   ____

| bought | caught | thought | fought |
| taught | daughter | ought | brought |

Fill in each blank with a word from the box.

1. Carlos _________________ a shirt at the store.
2. I _________________ a bad cold.
3. I _________________ you were not going to do that again.
4. The teacher _________________ fifth grade math.
5. A girl born to a mother is the mother's _________________.
6. Steve _________________ his dog to the vet.
7. You _________________ not cross the street here.
8. The two siblings _________________ constantly.

Fill in the blanks with either *ought* or *aught*.

1. We f_________ to save the town park.
2. My teacher's d_________er came to visit the class.
3. I th_________ long and hard about the question.
4. You _________ to go inside now for dinner.
5. We br_________ a pumpkin pie for dessert.
6. I t_________ my little sister how to read.
7. Mom c_________ ten fish at the lake.
8. Brit b_________ a ticket to the opera.

S.P.I.R.E.® Level 6 © SSI • Do Not Copy

Circle the *ought* and *aught* words and write them on the lines below.

1. The teacher taught a math lesson.
2. The couple was with their daughter.
3. The two friends bought gifts for each other.
4. The teacher taught a lesson on spelling.
5. The child brought his lunch to school.
6. The baseball player caught the ball.
7. The football player caught the pass.
8. The child brought the rabbit to school.
9. The baseball player caught a cold.
10. Dad brought Nana some flowers.
11. Alma sought her step-sister's advice.
12. Rob and his brother never fought about whose turn it was to walk the dog.
13. The trip across the sea was fraught with risk.
14. "You ought to study for the math test," said Aman.
15. Who taught you to ride a bike?

________________________   ________________________

________________________   ________________________

________________________   ________________________

________________________   ________________________

________________________   ________________________

________________________   ________________________

________________________   ________________________

S.P.I.R.E.® Level 6 © SSI • Do Not Copy

A Rose Is a Rose

1. What was Mrs. Sweet's problem?

2. How did Mrs. Sweet attempt to solve the problem?

3. What did Mrs. Snag mean when she said, "Now she has the biggest thorn of her life"?

4. What was Rose's problem?

S.P.I.R.E.® Level 6 © SSI • Do Not Copy

5. What changed the way Rose was acting?

____

____

____

6. Did Mrs. Snag's plan work?

____

____

____

Haughty means "scornfully proud." Other words that mean the same thing as *haughty* are: *arrogant, disdainful,* and *overbearing*.

7. Write three examples from the story that show how Rose was haughty.

____

____

____

____

____

S.P.I.R.E.® Level 6 © SSI • Do Not Copy

Match the rhymes.

thought	you
daughter	should
good	alone
stay	brave
night	being
true	day
seeing	brother
cave	taught
mother	water
phone	right

Write a rhyme for each word.

might   _________________

bike   _________________

ought   _________________

tray   _________________

naughty   _________________

snore   _________________

water   _________________

call   _________________

other   _________________

drone   _________________

S.P.I.R.E.® Level 6 © SSI • Do Not Copy

The Boy Who Thought Friends Could Be Bought

1. Why do you think Dilbert's mother and father gave him whatever he wanted?

   ____

   ____

2. How did having everything he wanted turn out to be a problem for Dilbert?

   ____

   ____

3. When did Dilbert first have a problem at school?

   ____

   ____

4. What happened after Dilbert gave a bribe to his classmates?

   ____

   ____

5. What happened to solve Dilbert's problem?

   ____

   ____

6. What lesson did Dilbert learn?

   ____

   ____

   ____

S.P.I.R.E.® Level 6 © SSI • Do Not Copy

Write the past form of the words below.

teach   __________________

buy   __________________

catch   __________________

think   __________________

fight   __________________

bring   __________________

Write a word or phrase that means the same thing as each word below.

ought   ______________________________

fought   ______________________________

haughty   ______________________________

taught   ______________________________

Write four sentences using the words above.

1. ______________________________________

   ____

2. ______________________________________

   ____

3. ______________________________________

   ____

4. ______________________________________

   ____

S.P.I.R.E.® Level 6 © SSI • Do Not Copy

Peace Begins

1. What did the bully think he needed to do differently? Write the line from the poem below.

____

____

2. What did he learn about fighting?

____

____

3. How do you think he found the strength to stop fighting?

____

____

4. How did the bully feel after he stopped fighting?

____

____

5. List three things you could do each day to keep peace in your school.

____

____

____

| fuel | clue | dueled | flue | glue |
| rescue | argue | fondue | tissue | barbeque |

Write the word on the line.

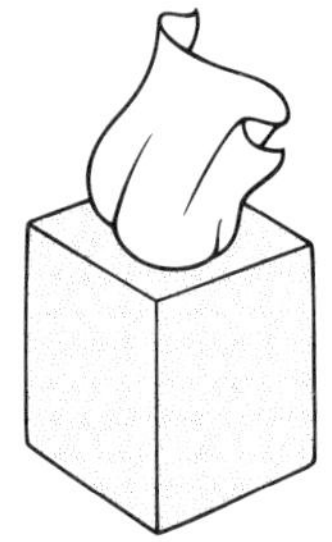

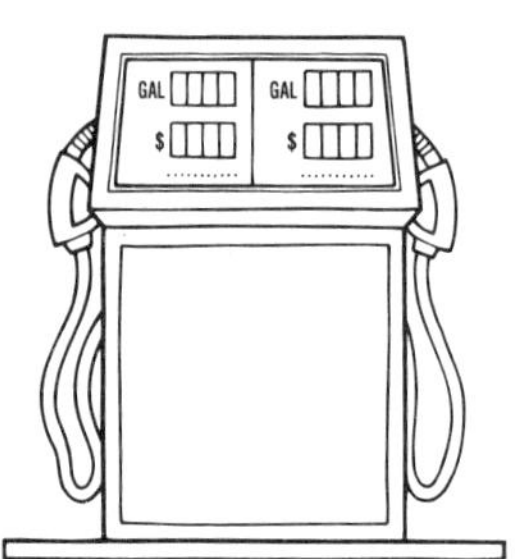

____

____

____

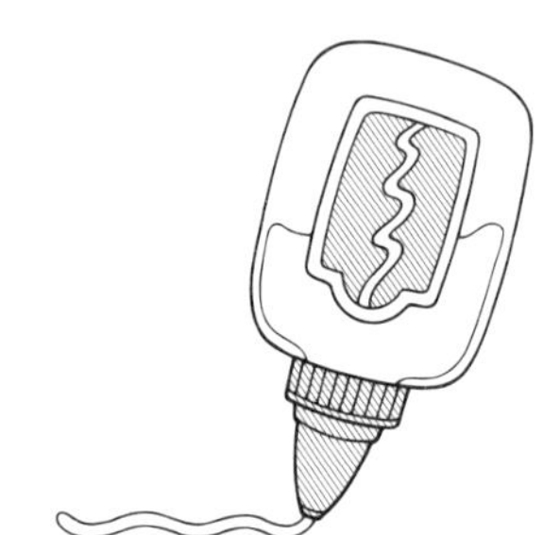

____

____

____

Fill in each blank with a word from the box.

1. I like to eat cheese _________________.

2. Please do not _________________ with me!

3. The chess players _________________ all afternoon.

S.P.I.R.E.® Level 6 © SSI • Do Not Copy

grew	few	new	news
flew	crew	chew	screw
sewer	blew	threw	stew

Write the word on the line.

____

____

Fill in each blank with a word from the box.

1. The rain ran down into the _________________.

2. Dan tightened a loose _________________ on the door hinge.

3. The tall tree _________________ from a seed.

S.P.I.R.E.® Level 6 © SSI • Do Not Copy

<table>
<tr><td>spatula</td><td>punctual</td><td>virtue</td><td>statue</td></tr>
<tr><td>congratulate</td><td>fortune</td><td>tarantula</td><td>mutual</td></tr>
</table>

32

Write the word on the line.

____

____

____

____

Fill in each blank with a word from the box.

1. The railroad tycoon made his _________________ in the railroad business.

2. Patience is a _________________, a good trait to have.

3. We made the decision together, so it was a _________________ decision.

4. Someone who is never late is a _________________ person.

Read these words and their meanings.

pursue	go after with strong intent
fortune	fate, destiny; riches
shrewd	keen awareness and sense of the practical
punctual	on time
perpetual	lasting for a long time; continuing
fluctuate	to change or not be regular
actual	real; a fact
strew	to scatter
virtue	moral excellence; goodness
mutual	given and received in equal amount, possessed in common

Replace the underlined word(s) in each sentence with a word from the box.

shrewd	pursued	punctual	strewn	mutual

1. Jackie Robinson <u>went after</u> the chance to play baseball.

   ____

2. Dad was always <u>on time</u>. _______________

3. The room was <u>scattered</u> with books. _______________

4. Our respect for each other was <u>given and received in equal amounts</u>. _______________

5. He is <u>very practical and has a keen awareness</u>. _______________

S.P.I.R.E.® Level 6 © SSI • Do Not Copy

Pursue Your Dreams

Summarize what each person did to pursue his or her dream.

Louis Pasteur

____

____

____

____

Helen Keller

____

____

____

____

Jackie Robinson

____

____

____

____

S.P.I.R.E.® Level 6 © SSI • Do Not Copy

Draw a picture to illustrate each sentence.

<table>
<tr><td>Lewis had strewn socks all over his bedroom.</td><td>The dolphin statue stood in the flower garden.</td></tr>
<tr><td>A few bluebirds flew across the field.</td><td>Congratulations! You won the trophy!</td></tr>
</table>

The Statue of Liberty

1. How did the idea of the Statue of Liberty come about?

2. Who built the Statue of Liberty? How did the builder design the face of the statue?

3. What was the problem with constructing the actual full-scale model of the Statue of Liberty?

4. How was the statue sent to the United States?

5. What was the problem when the statue first arrived in the United States?

6. Why do you think the Statue of Liberty is important?

S.P.I.R.E.® Level 6 © SSI • Do Not Copy

Box the *ue, ew,* or *tu*. Then say the word and read its meaning.

statue	a figure made from stone, wood or other material
pursue	to seek, find, or obtain
shrewd	clever, aware, astute
mutual	shared by two or more
actual	true, real, not false

Choose a word from the box to replace the underlined word(s) in each sentence and write it on the line.

1. With tax, this is the <u>real</u> cost of the new bicycle.

   ____

2. I am glad Andrew is president. He has many <u>clever</u> ideas.

   ____

3. The <u>figure</u> was made of copper and brass. _______________

4. The agreement we made about chores was to our <u>shared</u> benefit.

   ____

5. Pam will <u>look for</u> a career in art. _______________

Choose a word from the box to complete each sentence.

1. We both know Jon Kim. He is a _______________ friend.

2. The _______________ of Liberty stands in New York Harbor.

3. Her _______________ common sense helped her solve many problems.

4. Tom will _______________ an internship in the mayor's office.

5. What are your _______________ feelings about the project?

S.P.I.R.E.® Level 6 © SSI • Do Not Copy

Hue Adds to His Virtues

1. List Hue Chang's virtues.

2. What was Hue's problem?

3. How do you know that Jewell was a shrewd friend?

4. How did Hue finally come to understand what he was doing to others?

S.P.I.R.E.® Level 6 © SSI • Do Not Copy

5. How did Hue solve his problem?

____

____

____

____

6. List four of your virtues. Explain each one in a complete sentence.

____

____

____

____

____

____

____

7. Make a plan of three things you could do next week to improve your weaknesses.

1) ____

____

2) ____

____

3) ____

____

S.P.I.R.E.® Level 6 © SSI • Do Not Copy

broil	poison	oil	noise
coil	coins	join	point
hoist	spoil	boil	foil

Write the word on the line.

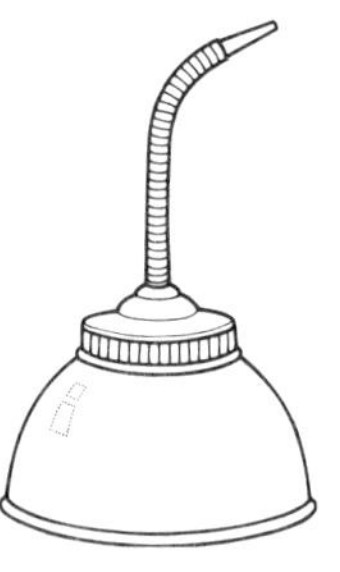

____

____

____

____

____

____

Fill in each blank with a word from the box.

1. Stop making so much _________________!

2. Will you _________________ me at the park?

3. The saying goes, "One man's meat is another man's _________________."

S.P.I.R.E.® Level 6 © SSI • Do Not Copy

<table>
<tr><td>cowboy</td><td>annoy</td><td>royal</td><td>convoy</td><td>oyster</td></tr>
<tr><td>loyal</td><td>joyful</td><td>soybean</td><td>destroy</td><td>toy</td></tr>
</table>

Write the word on the line.

____

____

____

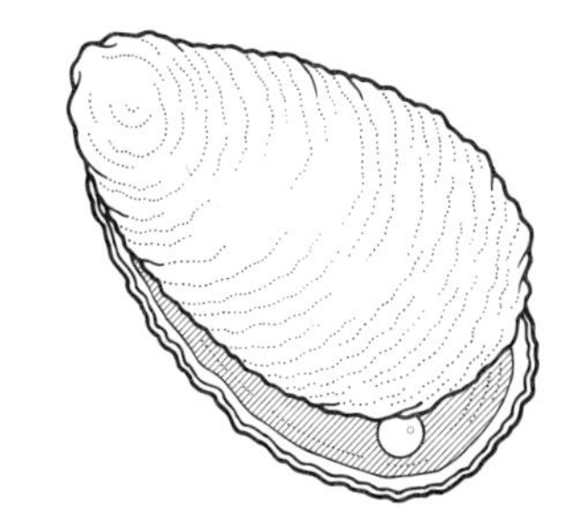

____

____

____

Fill in each blank with a word from the box.

1. Do not ________________ your little sister on purpose!

2. The wave will ________________ the sand castle.

3. ________________ can be made into tofu and soy milk.

S.P.I.R.E.® Level 6 © SSI • Do Not Copy

moist	annoyed	topsoil	avoid	hoist
spoil	employee	convince	pamphlet	princess
void	coil	voice	joy	loyal

Fill in each blank with a word from the box.

1. Dirt on top of the ground is called ___________________.

2. Someone who works for you is a(n) ___________________.

3. The daughter of a king is a ___________________.

4. To feel bothered by something is to be ___________________.

5. To get a person to believe something or do something is to

   ___________________ them.

6. A folded piece of paper with information inside is a

   ___________________.

7. Something just a little wet is ___________________.

8. A ___________________ is totally without or completely empty.

9. ___________________ is extreme happiness.

10. To pull up or lift is to ___________________.

11. To stay away from something is to ___________________ it.

12. To yell, you must raise your ___________________.

S.P.I.R.E.® Level 6 © SSI • Do Not Copy

The Ballad of Roy Royal

1. In the story Roy Royal is described as a "spinner of yarns." Explain what this means.

   ____

   ____

2. How did the children behave when Roy told stories?

   ____

   ____

3. What was one fault Roy had that led him to difficulty?

   ____

   ____

4. What was the result of Roy's problem?

   ____

   ____

5. Describe the stories that Roy tried to tell after his accident.

   ____

   ____

6. How did Roy change from the beginning of the story to the end?

   ____

   ____

Add *oy* or *oi* to make words. Then fill in the blank in each sentence with a word from the list.

r_________al   br_________l   sp_________l

cowb_________   s_________beans   m_________st

1. The dishcloth is not soaking wet; it is only _________________.

2. _________________s can be made into soy milk.

3. The king and queen are _________________.

4. Put the milk away or it will _________________.

5. The _________________ rode a big horse.

6. My dad will _________________ some fish for dinner.

oysters	bricks	corduroy	stew	fondue	nails
thread	screw	hammer	glue	soybeans	bread
cotton	wool	silk	velvet	wood	corn

List all the things clothing can be made of.

_________________   _________________   _________________

_________________   _________________   _________________

List foods.

_________________   _________________   _________________

_________________   _________________   _________________

List things to build with.

_________________   _________________   _________________

_________________   _________________   _________________

S.P.I.R.E.® Level 6 © SSI • Do Not Copy

Floyd Makes a Choice

1. What made Floyd a poor employee?

____

____

2. How did Miss Boyce try to help Floyd? What did her first warning say?

____

____

3. How did Floyd respond to Miss Boyce's warning?

____

____

4. What is a reference?

____

____

5. Write what you think Miss Boyce would say in a reference letter.

____

____

6. Why do employees ask for a reference?

____

____

7. What wise choice did Floyd finally make?

____

____

Read the meaning of each word.

hurl	to throw	**annoyed**	irritated
hoist	to lift	**noise**	many sounds
loyal	trustworthy	**rescue**	to save
destroy	demolish	**royal**	regal, like kings and queens
shrewd	keenly practical	**pointed**	extended a finger; with a sharp end

Use the words above to complete the story. Some words may be used more than once.

A grumpy giant lived on a cliff at the top of a steep mountain next to a small village. One day, the giant was ________________ by the joyful ________________ of the loud, happy villagers. "I will ________________ the town!" he said to himself. The giant began to ________________ large rocks at the people below.

The king and queen came out of their home to see what was going on. The villagers were very ________________ to the ________________ family, and wanted to keep them safe. "Look out!" said one child, as he ________________ up at the mountain.

Some people wanted to ________________ the giant, but the ________________ queen held them back. She suggested they get out of the way until the giant ran out of rocks or he became too tired to ________________ the rocks over his head.

Do you think the queen's plan worked? How would you ________________ the people from the giant?

S.P.I.R.E.® Level 6 © SSI • Do Not Copy

The City of Troy

1. Do we now believe that the city of Troy existed? How do we know? Was it ever discovered?

____

____

____

____

2. What were the people who lived in Troy called?

____

____

3. How many times was Troy rebuilt? How do we know?

____

____

____

4. What was the importance of the Trojan horse?

____

____

____

crawl	seesaw	pawn	paw	yawn
fawn	straw	claw	awning	hawk
draw	strawberry	jaw	shawl	flaw

Write the word on the line.

____

____

____

____

____

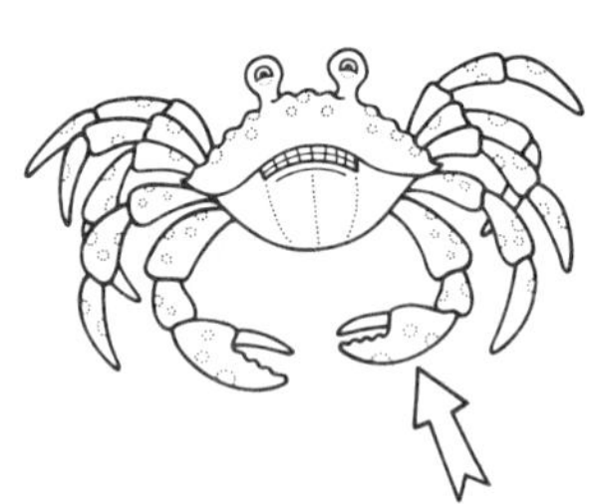

____

Fill in each blank with a word from the box.

1. Stand under the __________________ to stay dry in the rain.

2. Did you see the __________________ run through the woods?

3. My __________________ is sore from chewing gum.

S.P.I.R.E.® Level 6 © SSI • Do Not Copy

launch	laundry	gauze	saucer
applaud	vault	haul	autumn
gaunt	haunt	because	August

Write the word on the line.

_______________________   _______________________   _______________________

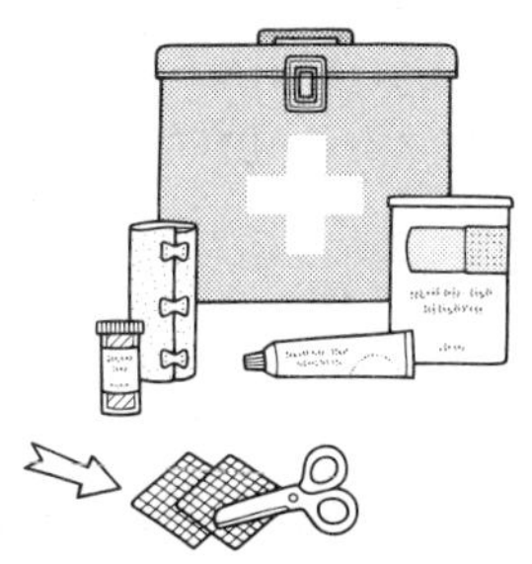

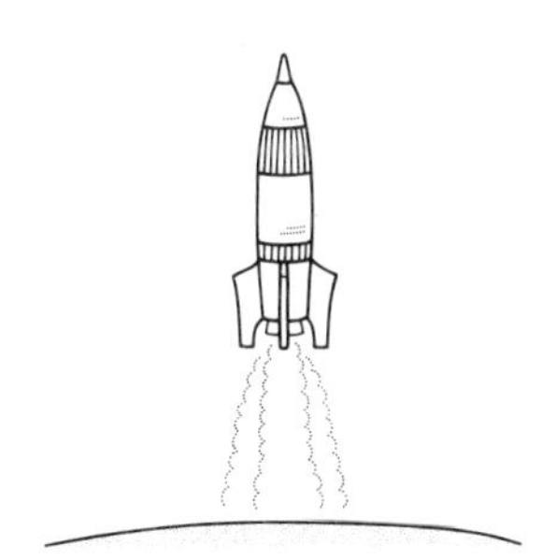

_______________________   _______________________   _______________________

Fill in each blank with a word from the box.

1. The cash is in the bank _______________________.

2. Did you wash your dirty _______________________?

3. The dump truck will _______________________ away the dirt.

4. Why did Molly go to the store? She went _______________________ she was out of milk.

Read these words and write them in the correct box.

autumn	angry	winter	stunned	peaceful
whisper	joyful	summer	spring	noise
crunch	ping	disappointed	shouts	thump
afraid	rumble	groan	enjoyment	buzz

Feelings

____

____

____

____

____

____

Sounds

____

____

____

____

____

____

____

Seasons

____

____

____

S.P.I.R.E.® Level 6 © SSI • Do Not Copy

Autumn

1. Name three trees in the poem.

2. List two *au* and two *aw* words from the poem.

3. How is autumn like an art show?

4. What does autumn represent to you?

5. Describe your favorite thing about autumn.

A Fair Trade

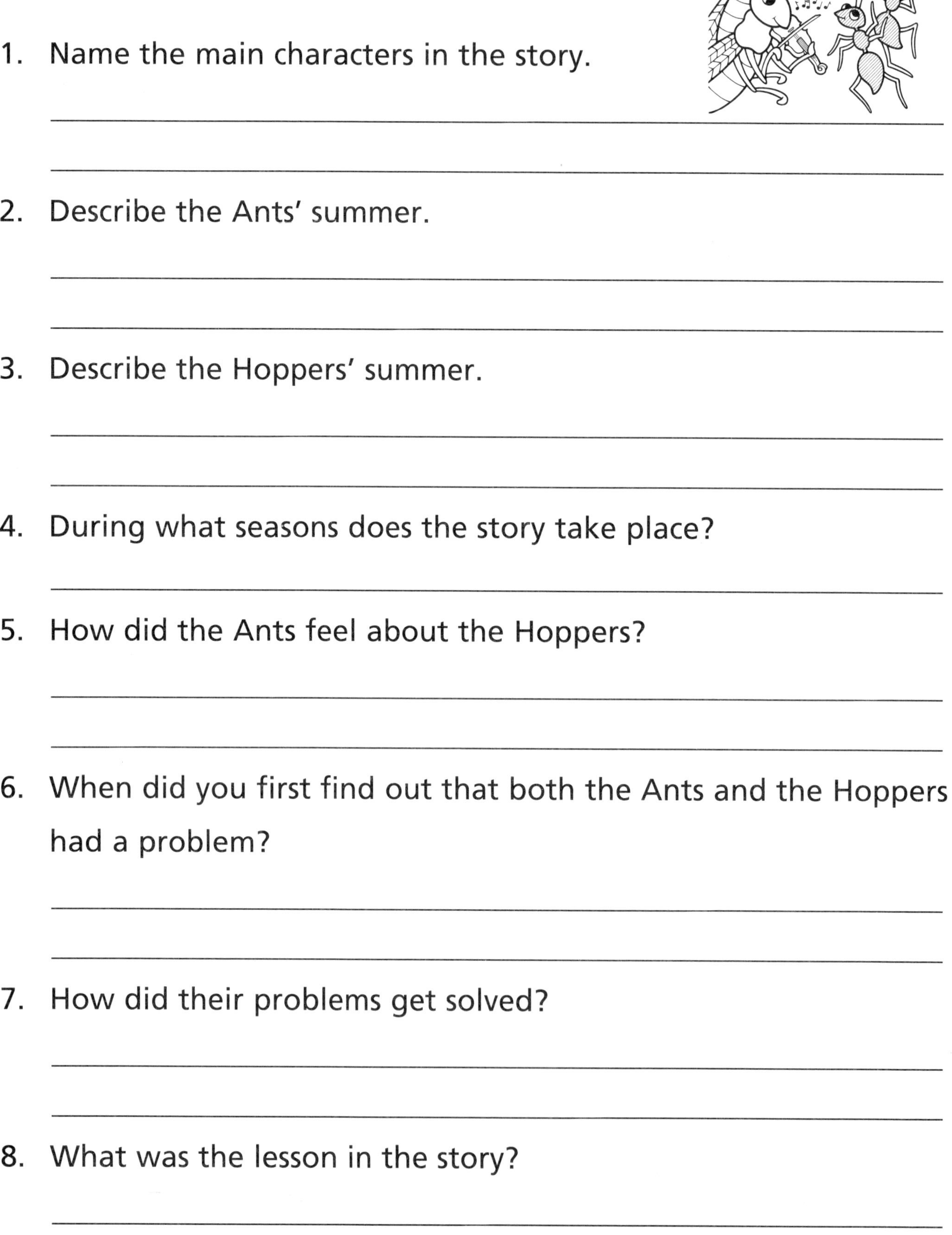

1. Name the main characters in the story.

2. Describe the Ants' summer.

3. Describe the Hoppers' summer.

4. During what seasons does the story take place?

5. How did the Ants feel about the Hoppers?

6. When did you first find out that both the Ants and the Hoppers had a problem?

7. How did their problems get solved?

8. What was the lesson in the story?

S.P.I.R.E.® Level 6 © SSI • Do Not Copy

Say the words and read their meanings.

flaunt	to show off
launch	to throw forward; hurl
dawn	sunrise; first daylight; the beginning of something
shawl	a covering of fabric for the head and shoulders
awning	a thin roof-like cover over a deck or window
vault	a room or compartment for storing valuables

Choose a word from the box to replace the underlined word(s) in the sentences.

1. _________________ Sue had a pretty <u>covering</u> over her shoulders.

2. _________________ The bank <u>compartment</u> held all the cash.

3. _________________ A(n) <u>roof-like cover</u> is over our deck.

4. _________________ I will meet you at <u>first daylight</u>.

5. _________________ We will watch the rocket <u>go forward and up</u> into orbit.

6. _________________ The girl should not <u>show off</u> her new ring.

Choose a word from above to finish each sentence.

1. Put anything of value in the _________________.

2. The sun is so bright we need a(n) _________________ to cover the window.

3. A new day will _________________.

4. If you are cold, you may borrow my _________________.

5. The rocket will _________________ into space.

6. It is rude to _________________ your riches.

S.P.I.R.E.® Level 6 © SSI • Do Not Copy

The Hawk

1. Discuss how the hawk is built for hunting.

    ____

    ____

2. Where is the one place in the world where you will not
    find hawks?

    ____

    ____

3. Name and describe the most common hawk in the United
    States.

    ____

    ____

4. How long does it take for a baby hawk to grow up?

    ____

    ____

S.P.I.R.E.® Level 6 © SSI • Do Not Copy

The word *launch* has several different meanings. Read the words in this web to find some words that have the same meaning.

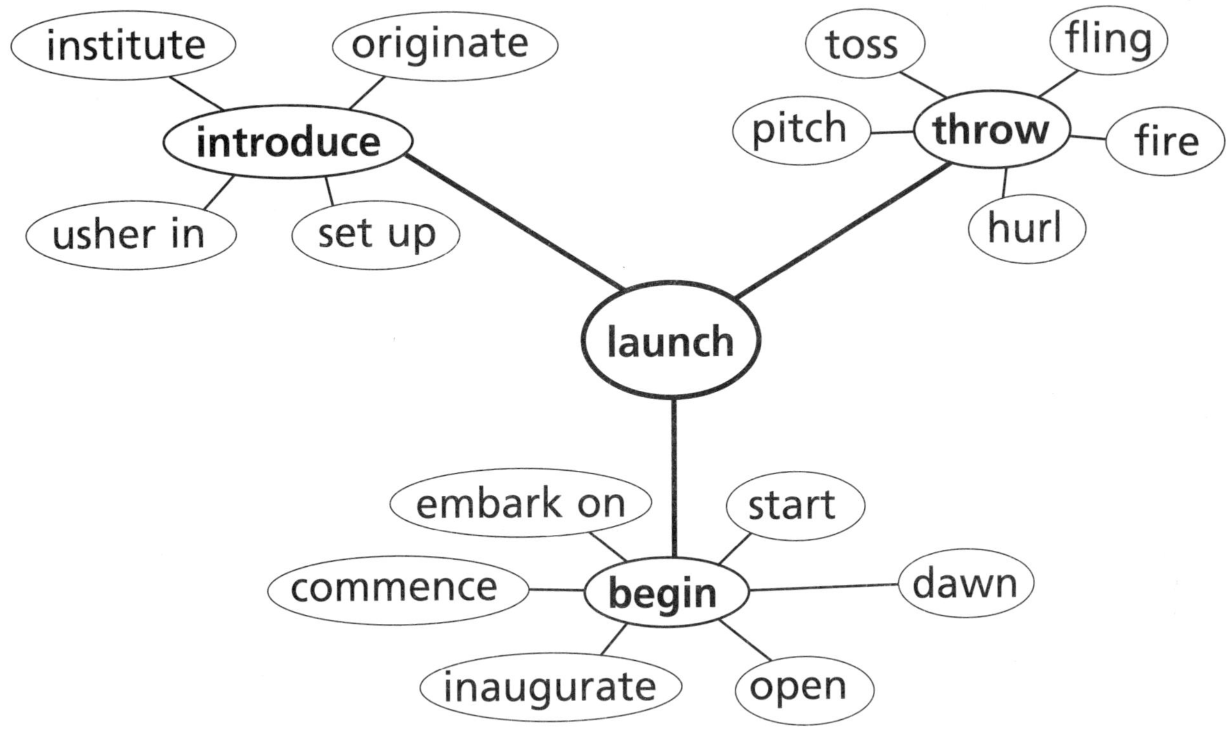

Choose two words from the diagram above to fill in the blanks below.

1. The child **launched** the toy out of the playpen. (throw)

   The child will ___________________ the toy out of the playpen.

   The child will ___________________ the toy out of the playpen.

2. We will **launch** the fundraising program tomorrow. (begin)

   We will ___________________ the fundraising program tomorrow.

   We will ___________________ the fundraising program tomorrow.

3. Sam had a meeting to **launch** his new plan. (introduce)

   Sam had a meeting to ___________________ his new plan.

   Sam had a meeting to ___________________ his new plan.

S.P.I.R.E.® Level 6 © SSI • Do Not Copy

 Circle all the things you might find in a bank.

interest
cash
photocopy

counter

stamp
vault

bankbook
advice

hawk

cash register
letters

point

pheasant
line

jail

thousands

checks

telephone

pamphlet

carpet

cloud

laundry

coins

fondue
author

soil

joint

raccoon

tellers

cell phone
windows

hive

teacher
manager

branches

drawers
hundreds

S.P.I.R.E.® Level 6 © SSI • Do Not Copy

Earthquakes

1. What are the three layers that make up the planet Earth?

   ____

   ____

2. What is a fault?

   ____

3. Where is the largest fault zone?

   ____

   ____

4. Approximately how many earthquakes are there a year? How many cause problems?

   ____

   ____

5. Discuss what we can do to protect ourselves from earthquakes.

   ____

   ____

   ____

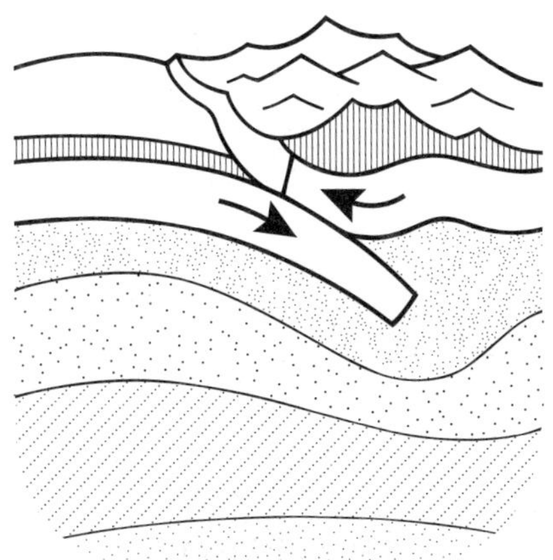

S.P.I.R.E.® Level 6 © SSI • Do Not Copy

| trolley | valley | key | monkey | hockey | turkey |
| chimney | pulley | money | volley | donkey | galley |

Write the word on the line.

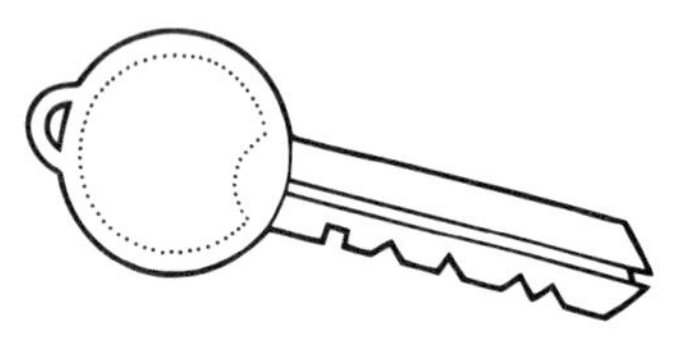

____

____

____

____

____

____

S.P.I.R.E.® Level 6 © SSI • Do Not Copy

Different spellings can make the long *a* sound. Write each word from the box under the correct spelling.

hey	hay	whey	prey	
stay	cape	train	mailbag	statement

ey   *ay*   *ai*   *a-e*

__________   __________   __________   __________

__________   __________   __________   __________

____

Different spellings can make the long *e* sound. Write each word from the box under the correct spelling.

volleyball	cream	Steve	turkey	please	tree

ey   *ea*   *ee*   *e-e*

__________   __________   __________   __________

__________   __________

S.P.I.R.E.® Level 6 © SSI • Do Not Copy

Honeybees

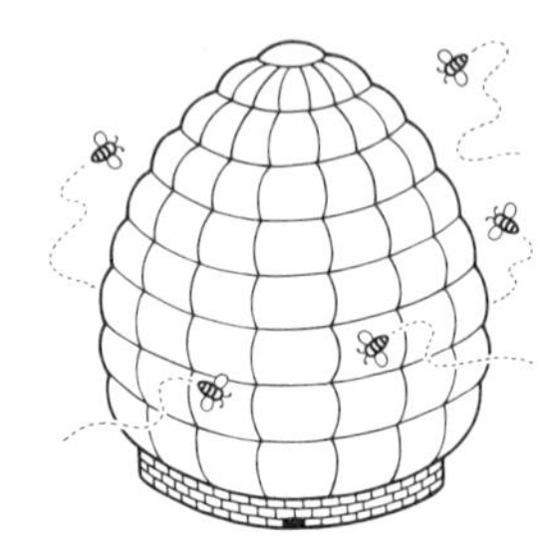

1. What are three key things that honeybees do?

____

____

____

2. List the members of a hive and what roles they play.

____

____

____

3. Discuss the worker bee, who changes her job. List the stages of her life.

____

____

____

____

4. What are three things a hive needs to survive?

____

____

5. What is a swarm?

____

____

S.P.I.R.E.® Level 6 © SSI • Do Not Copy

Mark the sentence as true or false, then find the sentence in the article *Honeybees* that supports your answer and write it under the statement.

T or F

____________   Honeybees are only found in the country.

____

____

____________   There are ten queen bees in every hive.

____

____

____________   The queen's job is to make more bees.

____

____

____________   Drones are male bees that live a long time.

____

____

____________   The worker bee is a female and lays eggs.

____

____

____________   Bees leave a hive when it is too full.

____

____

____________   The worker bee can sting many times.

____

____

S.P.I.R.E.® Level 6 © SSI • Do Not Copy

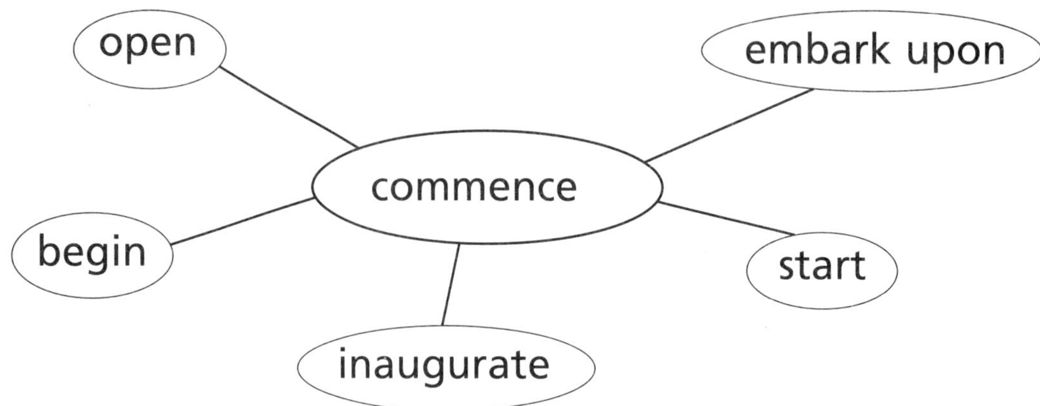

Fill in each blank with the correct *ey* word. Then rewrite the complete sentence, replacing *commence* with a word from the diagram meaning the same thing.

1. We will <u>commence</u> our long _________________ in the morning.

    ____

2. We will <u>commence</u> eating our _______________ at dinnertime.

    ____

3. We will <u>commence</u> pulling on the _______________ to move the heavy object.

    ____

4. The _______________ game will <u>commence</u> at 5:00.

    ____

5. _______________ said not to <u>commence</u> until we arrived.

    ____

6. Little Miss Muffet will <u>commence</u> eating her curds and _______________.

    ____

S.P.I.R.E.® Level 6 © SSI • Do Not Copy

The History of the Trolley Car in America

1. When and where were the first trolley lines established?

   ____

   ____

2. What was the problem with horse drawn trolleys?

   ____

   ____

3. Whose idea was the electric trolley?

   ____

   ____

4. How did the electric trolley run?

   ____

   ____

5. What was developed that made the trolley less used? Why was it more popular?

   ____

   ____

6. Do trolleys still exist? Write a sentence from the article that answers this question.

   ____

   ____

   ____

Read and illustrate each sentence.

The banker locked all the valuables in the vault.

On the warm autumn day, a swarm of bees looked like a black cloud.

Shirley's blue hockey jersey had the number thirteen written on it.

The hawk was perched high in the tree when it spotted the prey below.

S.P.I.R.E.® Level 6 © SSI • Do Not Copy

Valley Forge

1. Who is this article about?

____

2. What is a volunteer? What was the problem with the members of the Continental Army?

____

____

3. Why did General Washington choose Valley Forge to camp?

____

____

4. Describe the hardships at Valley Forge.

____

____

5. How long were the troops at Valley Forge before things began to get better? How did they get better?

____

____

6. The Continental Army did finally claim victory over the British. What happened to General George Washington?

____

____

<table>
<tr><td>write</td><td>knot</td><td>knob</td><td>wrestle</td><td>knight</td></tr>
<tr><td>wreath</td><td>wrist</td><td>knapsack</td><td>knife</td><td>knee</td></tr>
</table>

Write the word on the line.

____

____

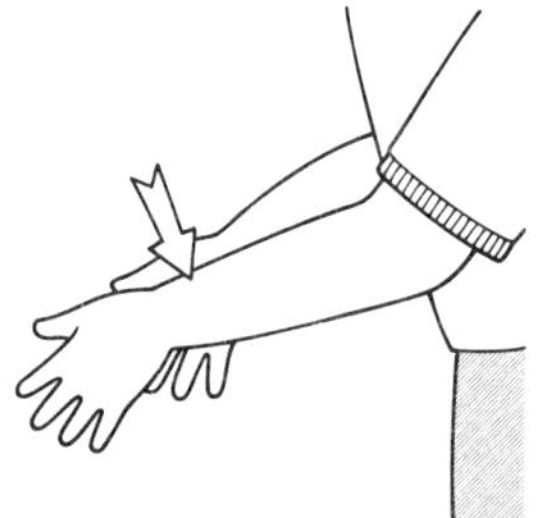

____

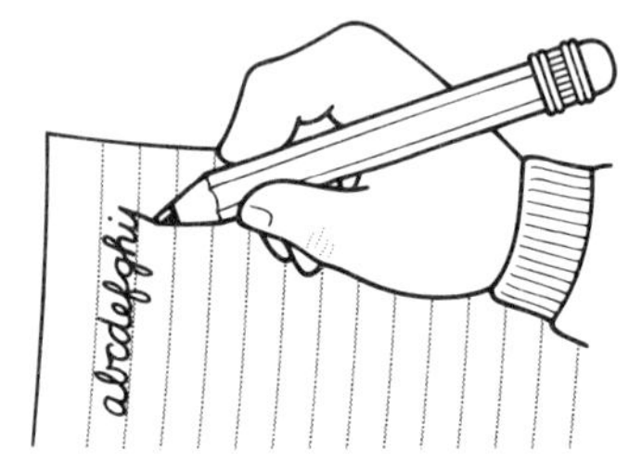

____

____

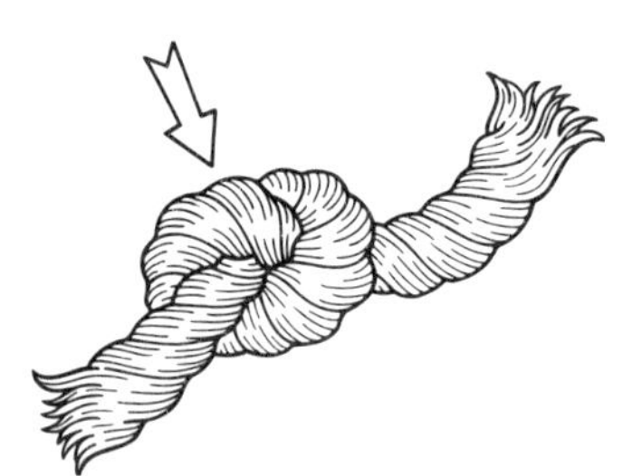

____

Fill in each blank with a word from the box.

1. The girls made a ____________________ out of wildflowers.

2. The two dogs play and ____________________.

3. Turn the ____________________ and open the door.

S.P.I.R.E.® Level 6 © SSI • Do Not Copy

<table>
<tr><td>thumb</td><td>guitar</td><td>comb</td><td>limb</td><td>spaghetti</td></tr>
<tr><td>guide dog</td><td>plumber</td><td>climb</td><td>guard</td><td>ghost</td></tr>
</table>

Write the word on the line.

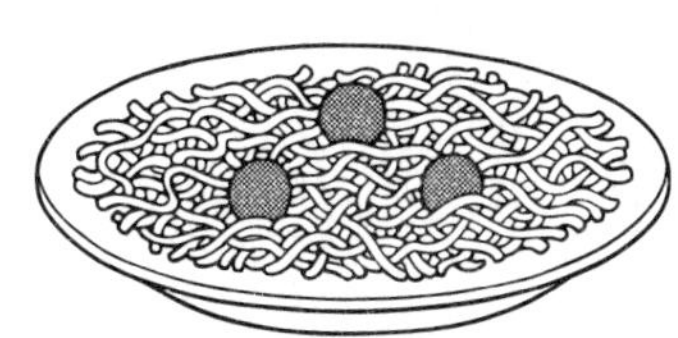

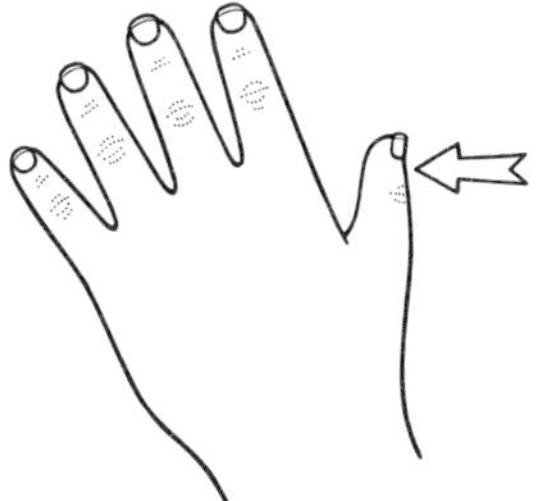

____

____

Fill in each blank with a word from the box.

1. Call the _________________ when the sink is clogged.

2. Do not hang on the tree _________________.

3. Let's _________________ up this steep hill.

S.P.I.R.E.® Level 6 © SSI • Do Not Copy

Some words sound the same but are spelled differently. Fill in each blank with the correct word.

knight   1. The squire became a(n) _______________.

night   2. It is very dark at _______________ when there is no moon.

knot   3. I will _______________ let you go until you finish your work.

not   4. The rope had a big _______________.

know   5. I _______________ that girl.

no   6. I said _______________ and I mean _______________!

knead   7. What do you _______________ to finish the job?

need   8. Mom will _______________ the bread dough to make it rise.

write   9. I will sit down and _______________ a letter.

right   10. Turn _______________ right at the next stoplight.

Choose a word from above that sounds the same.

night

____

need

____

right

____

no

____

not

____

S.P.I.R.E.® Level 6 © SSI • Do Not Copy

Knights

1. How are knights of today different from those of long ago?

____

____

2. List the three most important types of people during the Middle Ages, in order of their importance.

____

3. How did becoming a knight change during the 1100s?

____

____

4. When did a knight begin training?

____

____

5. Describe what a page was taught.

____

____

6. When did a page become a squire? What did a squire do?

____

____

7. Describe how knights acted.

____

____

S.P.I.R.E.® Level 6 © SSI • Do Not Copy

Fill in the blanks.

| write | knit | plumber | knife | limb |
| numb | knees | climb | spaghetti | wrapper |

1. Marvin's feet were so cold that they felt ________________.

2. We will ________________ Mount Everest next summer.

3. When the pipe broke, we called a(n) ________________.

4. A large ________________ broke off the tree during the storm.

5. We will have ________________ and meatballs for dinner.

6. The child fell off his bike and skinned his ________________.

7. Grandmother loves to ________________ sweaters.

8. The fork is on the left and the ________________ and spoon are on the right side of the plate.

9. I will sit down and ________________ a letter this evening.

10. The candy was in a bright red ________________.

S.P.I.R.E.® Level 6 © SSI • Do Not Copy

Ghost Crabs and Sand Dollars: A Florida Ecosystem

1. What is an intertidal zone?

____

____

2. What is a ghost crab?

____

____

3. What are two birds found along the shore in Florida? What do the birds leave behind that beachcombers are happy to collect?

____

____

____

4. Define "ecosystem."

____

____

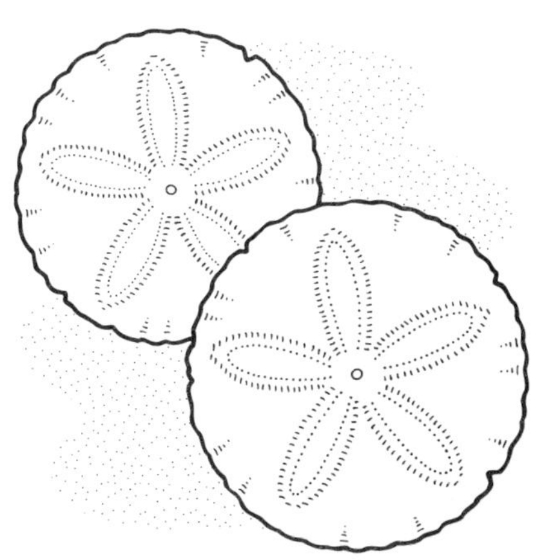

S.P.I.R.E.® Level 6 © SSI • Do Not Copy

Circle all the words for things you might find at a party.
Cross out what you think you would not find at a party.

string

spoons

oil

donkey

bricks

cake

clown

birds of prey

wrapping paper

ice cream

gifts

dolphins

flowers

shrew

shawls

soil

convoys

plates

balloons

knife

ribbon

ghost

wreaths

news

plumbers

hammers

guard

guide dog

combs

cards

knight

spaghetti

toys

knees

guests

schoolmates

knapsack

singing

popcorn

friends

S.P.I.R.E.® Level 6 © SSI • Do Not Copy

The Tomb of King Tut

1. When and where did Howard Carter make his discovery?

2. How do you think he felt at the beginning of the seventh try to find King Tut's tomb?

3. When Howard reached the door at the end of the tunnel, what did he find?

4. Who was George Herbert?

5. Who was King Tut?

6. Describe what was found when they opened the huge stone container holding King Tut's body.

7. Where are the artifacts found in King Tut's tomb now kept?

8. How long did it take Howard Carter to finish his work?

S.P.I.R.E.® Level 6 © SSI • Do Not Copy

| cabbage | bandage | cottage | luggage |
| garbage | message | postage | package |

Write the word on the line.

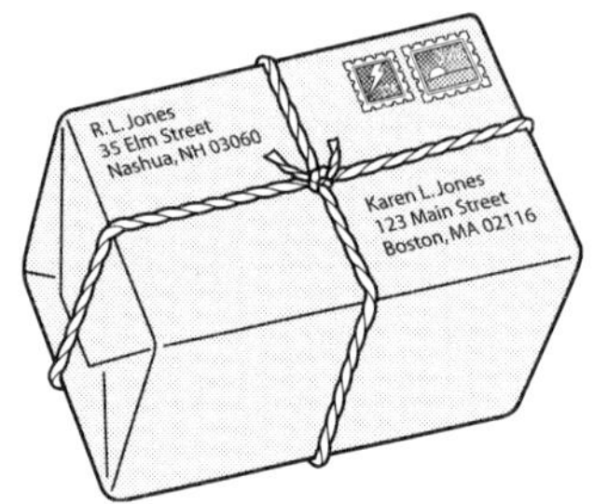

______________________   ______________________   ______________________

______________________   ______________________   ______________________

Fill in each blank with a word from the box.

1. The main ingredient in coleslaw is ______________________.

2. The ______________________ can is full and it smells bad.

3. The family stayed in a little ______________________ by the sea.

S.P.I.R.E.® Level 6 © SSI • Do Not Copy

Fill in the blanks.

rummage	storage	shortage	damage	cabbage
package	postage	luggage	voyage	garbage

1. The storm did a lot of _________________ to the trees.

2. The rabbit ate the _________________ in the garden.

3. We put the _________________ out on the curb on Tuesdays.

4. Dad went to the post office to ship the _________________.

5. The ship set out on a long _________________.

6. Mom bought new _________________ for the trip.

7. Trish and Max found lots of good used clothing at the _________________ sale.

8. There is a(n) _________________ of oil in our country.

9. The letter needed more _________________ to mail it.

10. Pablo kept his new lawnmower in the _________________ shed.

S.P.I.R.E.® Level 6 © SSI • Do Not Copy

The History of Mail

1. What is different between sending a message to someone now and one hundred years ago?

   ____

   ____

2. Why do you think a messenger who just memorized what someone wanted to say might not work well?

   ____

   ____

3. When did businesses first get involved with a postal system? Why?

   ____

   ____

4. Why was there a need for a public mail system?

   ____

   ____

5. What was the Penny Post? Explain where and how it began. Explain how it worked.

   ____

   ____

   ____

S.P.I.R.E.® Level 6 © SSI • Do Not Copy

6. Why did the British government begin to run the post? What was the problem?

____

____

____

7. Who was Rowland Hill? What idea of his is thought of as a milestone in the development of our postal system today?

____

____

8. What was the first British postage stamp called?

____

____

9. When was the first postage stamp issued in the United States? Describe it.

____

____

____

10. What happened in 1864 that made mail travel faster? How does mail now travel even faster?

____

____

____

S.P.I.R.E.® Level 6 © SSI • Do Not Copy

Read the words and their meanings.

voyage	a long journey, especially by sea
postage	a charge for mailing an item
cottage	a small dwelling, often in a rural setting
rummage	to search through trash for food or useful things
shortage	lacking; in need of

Fill in each blank with a word from above.

1. My sister will _________________ through my closet, looking for hand-me-downs.
2. The _________________ of qualified candidates made his job search easier.
3. My parents built a(n) _________________ in the woods.
4. The Penny Post in London first charged the public _________________ to send a letter.
5. The _________________ across the sea took ten days.

Fill in the correct word from the list above.

_________________   a long journey

_________________   a small house

_________________   the amount it costs to send a package

_________________   to search through to find something useful

_________________   not having enough

S.P.I.R.E.® Level 6 © SSI • Do Not Copy

The *Voyager* Spacecraft: Messages for Outer Space

1. What is the difference between a space probe and a spaceship?

   ____

   ____

2. Discuss the goals of *Voyager 1* and *Voyager 2*.

   ____

   ____

3. What did the space probes discover about Jupiter?

   ____

4. What did the *Voyagers* find out about Saturn?

   ____

   ____

5. Where are the *Voyagers* now?

   ____

   ____

6. What messages do both space probes carry?

   ____

   ____

7. If the *Voyagers* reach another planet, will we know what they discover?

   ____

   ____

Lewis and Clark and the Northwest Passage

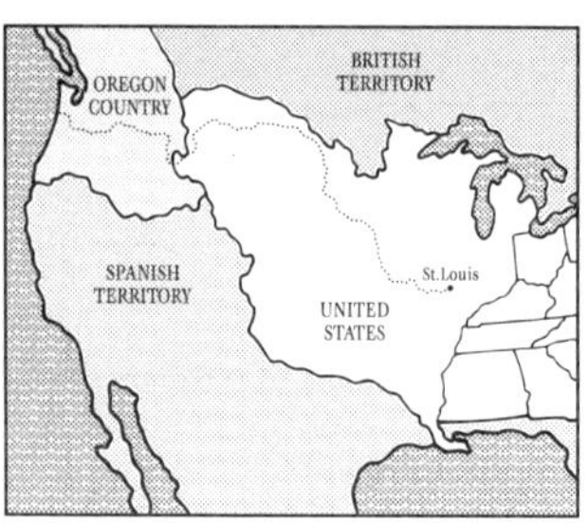

1. Which president decided to send explorers up the Missouri River to look for a Northwest Passage? What year was it?

____

____

2. Why did the United States want to do this?

____

____

3. Who were the explorers?

____

____

4. Why did the voyagers need great courage?

____

____

5. When did the explorers set out? Describe what it was like and some of the things they did.

____

____

____

S.P.I.R.E.® Level 6 © SSI • Do Not Copy

6. How did Sacagawea help the explorers?

____

____

____

7. Did they discover a Northwest Passage? How did they feel? Write the line from the article that answers this question.

____

____

____

8. Were Lewis and Clark considered successful explorers? Why or why not?

____

____

____

____

S.P.I.R.E.® Level 6 © SSI • Do Not Copy

Circle all the words that are related to Lewis and Clark and the Northwest Passage.

records

cabbage

Shoshone

Missouri River

garbage

Jefferson

upstream

mountains

luggage

circus

passage

postage

2,000 miles

shortage

rapids

damage

animals

wildlife

message

courage

beauty

village

maps

Pacific

storage

package

voyage

Sacagawea

dream

rummage

S.P.I.R.E.® Level 6 © SSI • Do Not Copy

<table>
<tr><td>skaters</td><td>baby</td><td>paper</td><td>baking</td><td>crater</td></tr>
<tr><td>table</td><td>volcano</td><td>label</td><td>raking</td><td>gravy</td></tr>
</table>

Write the word on the line.

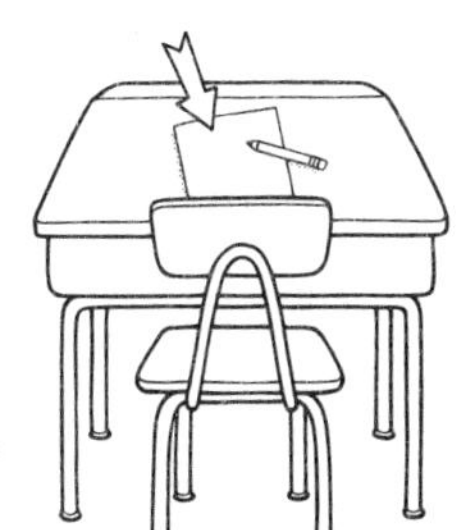

____

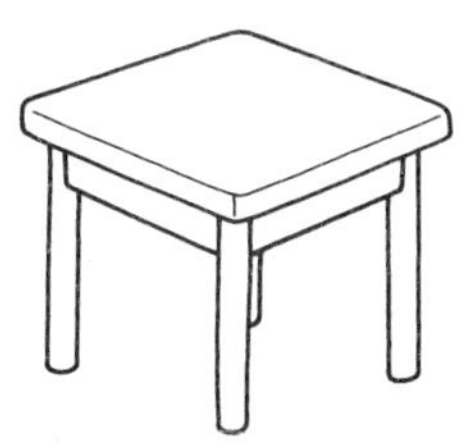

____

Fill in each blank with a word from the box.

1. Do you want ________________ on your turkey?

2. When a ________________ erupts, it spews lava.

3. Be sure to read the ________________ on the bottle.

S.P.I.R.E.® Level 6 © SSI • Do Not Copy

<table>
<tr><td>hikers</td><td>lion</td><td>pilot</td><td>violin</td><td>ivy</td></tr>
<tr><td>diving</td><td>spider</td><td>tiger</td><td>bicycle</td><td>sliding</td></tr>
</table>

Write the word on the line.

_______________   _______________   _______________

_______________   _______________   _______________

Fill in each blank with a word from the box.

1. Male _______________s have large brown manes.

2. Green _______________ vines grow on the side of our house.

3. The children at the playground were _______________ down the slide.

S.P.I.R.E.® Level 6 © SSI • Do Not Copy

<table>
<tr><td>oboe</td><td>open</td><td>over</td><td>pony</td><td>motor</td></tr>
<tr><td>potatoes</td><td>rodent</td><td>robot</td><td>sofa</td><td>molar</td></tr>
</table>

Write the word on the line.

____

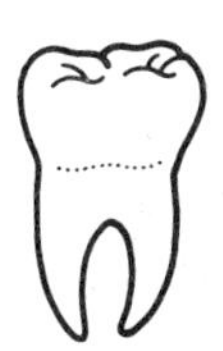

____

____

____

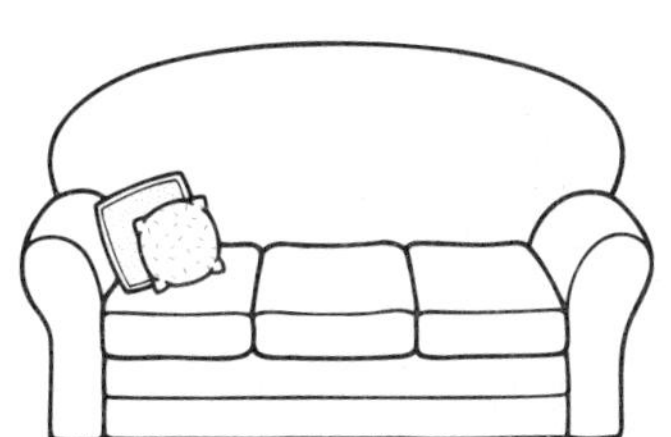

____

____

Fill in each blank with a word from the box.

1. Jessie plays the _________________ in the band.

2. The cow jumped _________________ the moon.

3. French fries are made from _________________.

music	cucumber	tuba	tuna	tulip
student	flutist	human	museum	hula

Write the word on the line.

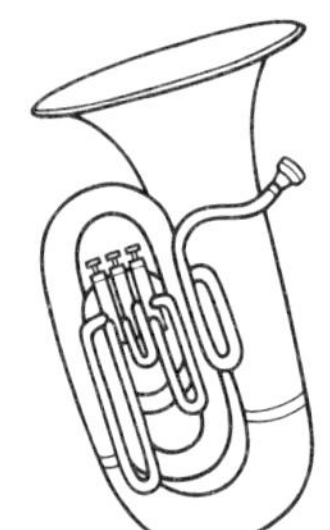

____

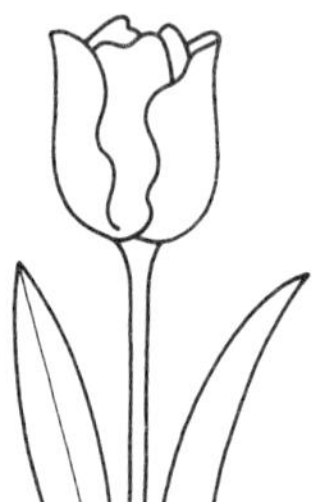

____

Fill in each blank with a word from the box.

1. Would you like a _________________ fish sandwich?

2. There are more than 200 bones in the _________________ body.

3. The class took a trip to the history _________________.

4. Tom trained his dog to jump through a _________________ hoop.

S.P.I.R.E.® Level 6 © SSI • Do Not Copy

<table>
<tr><td>lemur</td><td>eraser</td><td>even</td><td>zero</td><td>meter</td></tr>
<tr><td>recess</td><td>fever</td><td>female</td><td>hero</td><td>zebra</td></tr>
</table>

Write the word on the line.

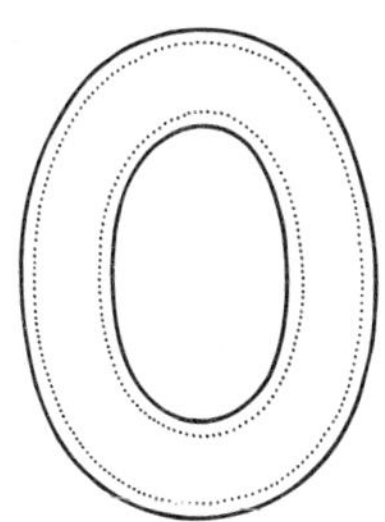

____

____

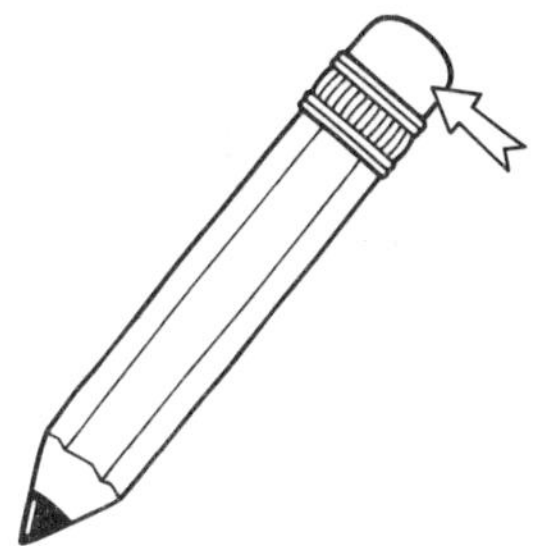

____

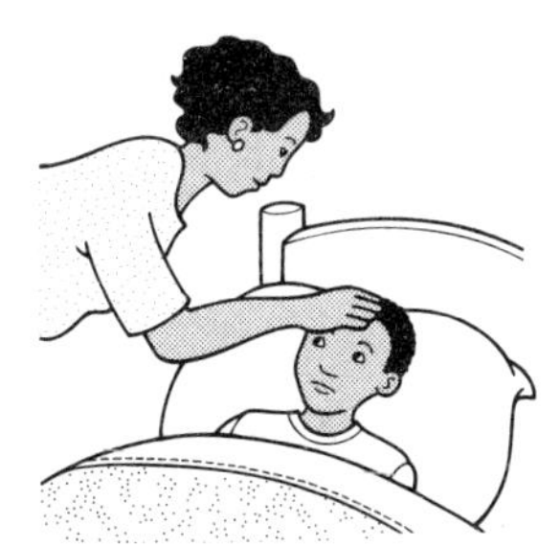

____

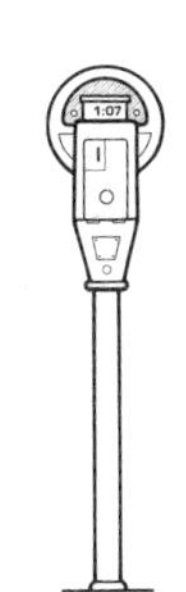

____

2, 4, 6, 8, 10 . . .

____

Fill in each blank with a word from the box.

1. During _________________, all the students played on the playground.

2. The good prince is usually the _________________ of the fairy tale.

3. Brothers are male and sisters are _________________.

4. The _________________ is a relative of the monkey.

S.P.I.R.E.® Level 6 © SSI • Do Not Copy

Underline all the vowels in the word. Put your two index fingers under the first two vowels. If there is one consonant between the vowels, you usually break the word apart after the first vowel.

Break apart these words. The first one is done for you.

pony   _____po_____   _____ny_____

robot   ___________   ___________

tiger   ___________   ___________

cucumber   ___________   ___________   ___________

baby   ___________   ___________

gravy   ___________   ___________

python   ___________   ___________

music   ___________   ___________

tornado   ___________   ___________   ___________

silent   ___________   ___________

S.P.I.R.E.® Level 6 © SSI • Do Not Copy

The Spider

1. How are spiders misunderstood?

   ____

   ____

2. Name two places where spiders cannot live. Tell why.

   ____

   ____

3. How do spiders eat their prey?

   ____

   ____

4. How many eggs do most spiders lay at once?

   ____

   ____

5. How are spiders helpful to humans?

   ____

   ____

S.P.I.R.E.® Level 6 © SSI • Do Not Copy

A Tale of King Midas

1. How did King Midas happen to meet Silenius?

2. What did Dionysus say when he appeared to thank King Midas for taking such good care of Silenius?

3. Why did King Midas wish for gold?

4. When did King Midas first discover his wish had caused a problem?

5. How was the wish broken?

6. How did the king's life change?

7. What does it mean today if someone is described as having "the Midas touch"?

S.P.I.R.E.® Level 6 © SSI • Do Not Copy

Read these words and their meanings.

carnivore	a flesh eating animal
spinnerets	a structure from which spiders and silkworms secrete silk threads to form webs or cocoons
provoke	to cause anger or resentment
burrow	a hole or tunnel dug in the ground by an animal for shelter
protect	to keep from damage or danger
detest	to dislike intensely

List three of each:

Carnivores

____

____

____

Foods you detest

____

____

____

Animals that burrow

____

____

____

Things that can provoke someone

____

____

____

Is Pluto Really a Planet?

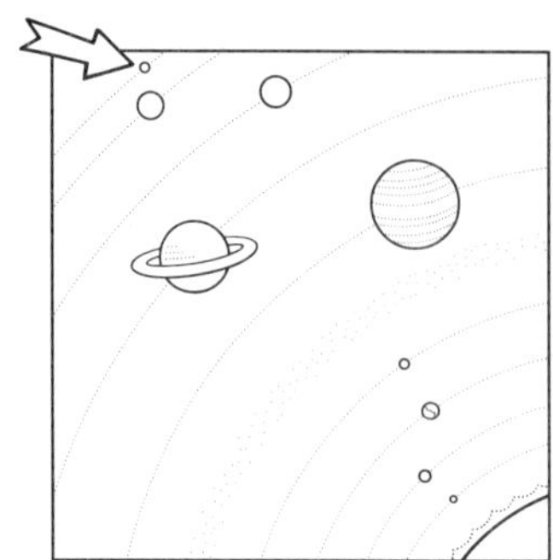

1. Who was Percival Lowell?

   ____

   ____

2. When was Pluto introduced as a planet?

   ____

   ____

3. How was the name Pluto chosen?

   ____

   ____

4. Why do some scientists feel Pluto is not a planet? Discuss
   three reasons.

   ____

   ____

5. Why do some scientists say Pluto is a planet?

   ____

   ____

6. What do you think?

   ____

   ____

S.P.I.R.E.® Level 6 © SSI • Do Not Copy

Put the planets back together.

Plu to   _______________________________

Ve nus   _______________________________

Mer cur y   _______________________________

Sa turn   _______________________________

Ju pi ter   _______________________________

Nep tune   _______________________________

U ra nus   _______________________________

Mars   _______________________________

Earth   _______________________________

Write each word in the box with the correct number of syllables:

1. One Syllable

____

____

2. Two Syllables

____

____

____

____

3. Three Syllables

____

____

____